LUNCH & BRUNCH
C·O·O·K·B·O·O·K

by Barbara Grunes

Ideals Publishing Corp.
Nashville, Tennessee

· Contents ·

Director of Publishing Patricia Pingry
Managing Editor Marybeth Owens
Cookbook Editor Naomi Galbreath
Art Director William Scholz
Photographer Gerald Koser
Editorial Assistant Linda Robinson
Typography Kim Kaczanowski

ISBN 0-8249-3042-8
Copyright © MCMLXXXV by Ideals Publishing Corp.
All rights reserved.
Printed and bound in the United States of America.

Published by Ideals Publishing Corporation
11315 Watertown Plank Road
Milwaukee, Wisconsin 53226
Published simultaneously in Canada

Cover Recipe
California Omelet, 21

BEVERAGES

Brunch Punch

Makes 20 servings

6 quarts black coffee at room
  temperature
¾ cup sugar or to taste
1 tablespoon vanilla
½ teaspoon nutmeg
½ teaspoon cinnamon
1 quart heavy cream
1 quart coffee ice cream
1 quart vanilla ice cream

In a punch bowl, stir together coffee and sugar until sugar dissolves. Stir in vanilla and spices. In a separate bowl, beat heavy cream until soft peaks form. Blend cream into coffee. Break ice cream into pieces with a spoon; add to coffee mixture.

Tea Punch

Makes 24 servings

2 cups strong tea
4 cups ginger ale
2 cups orange juice
2 cups cranberry juice
2 cups apple juice
  Sugar to taste
  Orange slices
  Pineapple chunks

Just before serving, stir together first 6 ingredients. Pour over an ice block in a punch bowl. Garnish with orange slices and pineapple chunks.

Egg Nog

Makes 12 servings

10 eggs, separated
1½ cups sugar
1 quart milk
½ cup heavy cream
½ teaspoon vanilla
¾ cup brandy
1 cup light rum
  Nutmeg

In a large mixing bowl, beat egg yolks until foamy. Add sugar; continue beating until mixture is lemon-colored. Stir in milk and cream. With clean beaters, beat egg whites in a separate bowl until stiff. Gradually beat in vanilla, then brandy and rum. Fold into milk mixture. Sprinkle with nutmeg.

Tomato Energizer

Makes 8 servings

4 eggs
4 cups tomato juice
½ teaspoon salt
½ teaspoon Worcestershire
 sauce
Dash Tabasco sauce

In a mixing bowl or blender, beat together all ingredients just until blended.

Cappucino

Makes 4 servings

2 cups very strong coffee
2 cups milk
2 tablespoons sugar
Cinnamon
Nutmeg

In a medium saucepan over medium heat, bring coffee, milk, and sugar to a simmer. Remove from heat. Beat until mixture is foamy. Pour into individual coffee cups. Sprinkle with cinnamon and nutmeg.

Mint Julep

Makes 1 serving

6 mint leaves
1 teaspoon powdered sugar
2 teaspoons water
2¼ ounces bourbon
Orange slice
Mint sprig

Place mint leaves in a 12-ounce tumbler. Add sugar and water; stir until sugar dissolves. Add bourbon and enough ice to fill the tumbler. Stir until outside of tumbler is frosted. Garnish with an orange slice and a sprig of mint.

Sangria

Makes 6 servings

2 cups fresh orange juice
8 tablespoons fresh lemon juice
5 tablespoons superfine sugar
Ice cubes
Club soda
Dry red wine
¼ cup Maraschino cherries
6 orange slices

In a small bowl, stir together orange juice, lemon juice, and sugar until blended. Pour equal amounts of the juice mixture into 6 ice-filled glasses. Fill ⅔ full with club soda. Add dry red wine to taste. Garnish each serving with cherries and an orange slice.

BREADS

Pecan Rolls

Makes 1 dozen rolls

½ cup milk
4 tablespoons butter
⅓ cup granulated sugar
½ teaspoon salt
1 large egg at room
  temperature, lightly beaten
1 package active dry yeast
1 teaspoon granulated sugar
¼ cup warm water (105 to
  115° F)
2½ to 3 cups all-purpose flour

3 tablespoons melted butter
1 teaspoon cinnamon
6 tablespoons granulated sugar
½ cup packed brown sugar
1 cup chopped pecans

In a saucepan, scald milk. Add the 4 tablespoons butter, sugar, and salt; stir until butter melts. Cool to room temperature. Stir in egg; set aside. In a small bowl, dissolve yeast and sugar in water. Set aside for about 5 minutes. In a mixing bowl, combine milk mixture and yeast mixture; blend well. Stir in 1 cup of the flour. Gradually work in remaining flour until dough holds together. Turn dough out onto a lightly floured surface. Knead until smooth. Place dough in a greased bowl; turn to grease top. Place in a warm, draft-free area to rise until doubled in bulk, about 1½ hours.

Preheat oven to 375° F. Turn dough out onto a lightly floured surface. Roll out to an 8 x 16-inch rectangle. Brush the top with melted butter. Sprinkle cinnamon and sugar evenly over dough. Roll up jelly roll style. Cut into 12 pieces. Generously grease a 12-cup muffin pan. Sprinkle brown sugar and pecans into the bottom of each cup. Top with round of dough. Cover and let rise for 30 minutes in a draft-free area. Bake for 15 minutes. Turn rolls out onto a baking rack to cool.

Ham Fritters

Makes 6 to 8 servings

1 cup all-purpose flour
1 teaspoon baking powder
½ teaspoon salt
2 eggs, lightly beaten
1 cup minced cooked ham
¼ cup milk
  Peanut oil

In a deep bowl, combine flour, baking powder, and salt. In a separate bowl, beat together eggs, ham, and milk. Add to dry ingredients all at once; stir just until blended. Set aside for 20 minutes. In a deep skillet or saucepan, heat oil to 375° F. Slide batter by tablespoonfuls into hot oil. Fry 4 at a time. Cook until golden brown on all sides. Drain on paper towels.

Soft Rolls

Makes 2 dozen rolls

1 package active dry yeast
1 cup warm water (105-115° F)
½ cup sugar
½ teaspoon salt
1 egg, lightly beaten
½ cup vegetable shortening
3 cups all-purpose flour
1 tablespoon butter, melted and cooled

In a small bowl, dissolve yeast in warm water; set aside for 5 minutes. Stir in sugar, salt, and egg. In a large mixing bowl, beat together shortening and yeast mixture until blended. Gradually add flour, 1 cup at a time; beat until flour is absorbed and dough holds together. Turn dough out onto a lightly floured surface. Roll to a ¼-inch thickness. Cut into rounds with a 3-inch cookie cutter. Arrange rounds on baking sheet. Brush with melted butter, fold in half, and pinch edges to seal. Cover lightly with a kitchen towel. Set aside to rise until rolls have doubled in bulk, about 45 minutes. Preheat oven to 350° F. Bake for 12 to 15 minutes. Immediately remove from pans; cool on a rack.

English Scones

Makes 24 scones

1½ cups all-purpose flour
1½ cups cake flour
4 tablespoons sugar
2 tablespoons baking powder
6 tablespoons butter at room temperature
½ cup raisins
1 cup milk

Preheat oven to 400° F. Cover 2 baking sheets with parchment paper. In a large mixing bowl, stir together all-purpose flour, cake flour, sugar, and baking powder. Blend in butter; stir in raisins. Add milk; stir until well mixed. On a lightly floured surface, roll out dough to a ½-inch thickness. Cut with a 2-inch cookie cutter. Place scones on prepared baking sheets. Bake for 15 minutes or until light brown. Split scones and serve warm with butter and jam.

Bacon Corn Bread

Makes 8 servings

1½ cups yellow cornmeal
1 cup all-purpose flour
⅓ cup sugar
3 strips bacon, crisp-cooked and crumbled
1 tablespoon baking powder
½ teaspoon salt
2 eggs
1½ cups milk
4 tablespoons bacon drippings

Preheat oven to 400° F. Grease a 9-inch square baking pan or cornbread pan. In a mixing bowl, stir together cornmeal, flour, sugar, bacon, baking powder, and salt. In a separate bowl, beat eggs, milk, and 4 tablespoons bacon drippings until blended. Add to dry ingredients. Stir just until dry ingredients are moistened. Pour into prepared pan. Bake for 30 minutes or until a wooden pick inserted near the center comes out clean.

Panettone

Makes 1 loaf

2 packages active dry yeast
1 tablespoon sugar
½ cup warm water (105-115° F)
3½ cups all-purpose flour
3 eggs
2 egg yolks
1 teaspoon vanilla
2 teaspoons grated lemon peel
2 teaspoons grated orange peel
¾ cup butter at room
   temperature
¾ cup dark raisins
¼ cup chopped candied orange
   peel
1 egg, lightly beaten

In a large mixing bowl, dissolve yeast with sugar in warm water; set aside for 5 minutes. Stir ½ cup of the flour into yeast; set aside in a warm place until doubled in volume. Beat in remaining flour, eggs, egg yolks, vanilla, and grated citrus peel. Turn dough out onto a lightly floured surface and knead until dough is soft and elastic, about 6 minutes. Gradually knead in butter. Knead in raisins and candied orange peel. Place dough in a lightly oiled bowl. Turn dough to oil top. Cover lightly with a towel and set aside until doubled in bulk, about 1½ hours.

Punch dough down and knead until smooth, about 5 minutes. Place in a greased 1-pound coffee can. Set aside until doubled in bulk, about 50 minutes. Brush top of dough with egg. Bake at 400° F for 10 minutes; reduce heat to 350° F and continue baking for 35 minutes or until golden brown. Cool 5 minutes in the can. Turn out onto a rack to cool completely.

Orange Yogurt Bread

Makes 1 loaf

½ cup butter
1½ cups sugar
2 eggs
1½ cups all-purpose flour
1½ teaspoons baking powder
½ teaspoon salt
½ cup orange juice
1 tablespoon grated orange peel
1 cup unflavored yogurt

Preheat oven to 350° F. Grease and flour a 9 x 5-inch loaf pan. In a large mixing bowl, cream butter and sugar until fluffy. Add eggs; beat well. In a separate bowl, stir together flour, baking powder, and salt. In a small bowl, combine orange juice, orange peel, and yogurt. Add dry ingredients to creamed mixture alternately with yogurt mixture. Pour batter into prepared pan. Bake for 55 minutes or until a wooden pick inserted near the center comes out clean. Cool in pan 10 minutes. Remove bread from pan and cool on a rack. Frost with Orange Icing while bread is still warm.

Orange Icing

¾ cup powdered sugar
4 tablespoons orange juice
1 tablespoon orange liqueur or
   Triple Sec

In a small bowl, combine sugar, orange juice, and liqueur; beat until mixture is smooth.

Spoon Bread

Makes 8 servings

1½ cups boiling water
1 cup cornmeal
1 tablespoon butter, melted
3 eggs, separated
1 cup buttermilk
1 teaspoon sugar
1 teaspoon baking powder
¼ teaspoon baking soda
½ teaspoon salt
Butter at room temperature

Preheat oven to 375° F. Grease a 2-quart casserole. In a large bowl, stir boiling water into cornmeal. To prevent lumping, stir until the mixture is cool. Blend in butter and egg yolks. Stir in buttermilk, sugar, baking powder, soda, and salt. Beat egg whites just until soft peaks form; fold into batter. Pour batter into prepared casserole; bake 45 to 50 minutes. Spoon onto a plate. Serve with butter; eat with a fork or spoon.

Orange Tea Bread

Makes 1 loaf

1 cup orange marmalade
2 eggs
1 cup fresh orange juice
2 tablespoons butter, melted
2¾ cups all-purpose flour
½ cup sugar
2 teaspoons baking powder
1 teaspoon baking soda
¼ teaspoon salt
¾ cup chopped walnuts
2 teaspoons grated orange peel
1 teaspoon grated lemon peel

Preheat oven to 350° F. Grease and flour a 9 x 5-inch loaf pan. In a mixing bowl, stir together marmalade, eggs, orange juice, and butter until blended. In a separate bowl, stir together flour, sugar, baking powder, soda, and salt. Add orange mixture; beat until smooth. Fold in nuts, orange peel, and lemon peel. Spoon batter into prepared pan; bake for 1 hour or until a wooden pick inserted near the center comes out clean. Cool in the pan for 10 minutes; turn out onto a rack to cool completely.

Summer Fall Muffins

Makes 12 muffins

2 cups all-purpose flour
½ cup granulated sugar
¼ cup firmly packed light brown sugar
1 tablespoon baking powder
1 teaspoon cinnamon
½ teaspoon salt
2 eggs
5 tablespoons vegetable oil
¾ cup milk
1½ cups dates *or* fresh cranberries

Preheat oven to 375° F. Grease a 12-cup muffin pan. In a mixing bowl, combine flour, sugars, baking powder, cinnamon, and salt. In a separate bowl, beat eggs, oil, and milk until well blended. Add egg mixture to flour mixture; beat just until batter is moistened. Stir in dates. Fill muffin cups ⅔ full. Bake for about 20 minutes. Remove muffins from pan immediately; cool on a wire rack.

Lemon Bread

Makes 1 loaf

1 cup butter *or* margarine
2 cups sugar
4 eggs
3 cups all-purpose flour
½ teaspoon salt
½ teaspoon baking soda
1 cup buttermilk
    Grated peel of 1 lemon
1 cup chopped walnuts
    Juice from 3 lemons
1 cup powdered sugar

Preheat oven to 350° F. Grease and flour a 9 x 5-inch loaf pan. In a mixing bowl, cream butter and sugar. Add eggs, 1 at a time, beating well after each addition. In a separate bowl, stir together flour, salt, and soda. Add dry ingredients to creamed mixture alternately with buttermilk. Stir in lemon peel and walnuts. Pour batter into prepared pan. Bake for 1 hour or until a wooden pick inserted near the center comes out clean. Cool bread in pan 10 minutes; turn out onto a rack to cool completely. To make glaze, combine lemon juice and powdered sugar. Pierce top of cooled bread with a fork several times. Drizzle glaze over bread.

Easy Onion Cake

Makes 8 servings

4 tablespoons butter
1 large onion, thinly sliced
1 8-ounce package refrigerator
    biscuits
1 egg
1 cup sour cream
½ teaspoon salt
2 teaspoons poppy seeds

Preheat oven to 375° F. In a large, heavy skillet over medium heat, melt butter. Add onion; sauté until tender. Arrange biscuits to cover the bottom of an ungreased 9-inch round cake pan. Spoon onion over biscuits. In a small bowl, beat egg with sour cream and salt; pour over onion. Sprinkle with poppy seeds. Bake for 30 minutes or until center is set.

Soda Bread with Raisins

Makes 1 loaf

3 cups all-purpose flour
¼ cup sugar
2 teaspoons baking powder
1 teaspoon baking soda
½ teaspoon salt
1 cup raisins
½ cup candied fruit, chopped
1¼ cups buttermilk
2 tablespoons vegetable oil

Preheat oven to 375° F. Grease a baking sheet. In a bowl, stir together flour, sugar, baking powder, soda, and salt. Stir in raisins and candied fruit. In a mixing bowl, beat buttermilk with oil until blended. Stir in flour mixture; beat until a soft dough forms. Turn dough out onto a lightly floured surface. Knead for 1 minute. On prepared baking sheet, shape dough into a round loaf. Bake for 40 minutes.

EGGS

Chicken Timbales

Makes 6 servings

1½ cups chopped cooked chicken
¾ cup shredded Cheddar cheese
1½ cups milk
6 eggs, lightly beaten
2 tablespoons instant minced
  onion
½ teaspoon salt
½ teaspoon paprika
3 teaspoons grated Parmesan
  cheese

Preheat oven to 350° F. Place 6 custard cups in a baking pan. Measure ¼ cup chicken and 2 tablespoons Cheddar cheese into each cup. Heat milk until just below simmering; set aside. In a mixing bowl, beat together eggs, onion, salt, and paprika. Stir milk into egg mixture until well blended. Pour egg mixture into custard cups. Sprinkle each cup with ½ teaspoon Parmesan cheese. Place baking pan in oven. Pour water into pan to within ½ inch of the top of custard cups. Bake until knife inserted near center of the custard comes out clean, about 25 minutes. Remove custard cups from hot water. Gently loosen custards with a spatula; invert onto serving plates.

Chived Cheese Omelet

Makes 2 servings

4 eggs
¼ cup water
1 tablespoons chopped chives
¼ teaspoon salt
  Dash white pepper
1½ tablespoons butter
½ cup shredded Cheddar cheese
  Chive flowers

In a mixing bowl, beat eggs with water, chives, salt, and pepper. In a 10-inch skillet, heat butter until it begins to sizzle. Pour in egg mixture. When edges set, tilt pan while lifting edges of omelet so that uncooked eggs flow to bottom of pan. While top of omelet is still moist and creamy, sprinkle ¼ cup of the cheese over half of the omelet. Fold omelet over cheese; turn out onto a platter. Top with remaining cheese. Garnish with chive flowers, if available.

Lunch in a Skillet

Makes 6 servings

3 to 4 slices bacon, diced
1 cup frozen Southern-style
  hash brown potatoes
¼ cup chopped onion
6 eggs
⅓ cup water
½ teaspoon salt
½ teaspoon dill

In a large skillet over medium heat, cook bacon until crisp. Transfer to paper towels to drain. Pour off all but 3 tablespoons drippings. Add potatoes and onion. Cook, stirring occasionally, until potatoes begin to brown, about 5 minutes. Beat eggs with water, salt, and dill; stir in bacon. Pour over potato mixture in skillet. Cook, stirring occasionally, until eggs are cooked through but still moist.

Eggs Benedict

Makes 8 servings

8 slices Canadian bacon
8 eggs
4 English muffins
  Hollandaise Sauce
  Orange slices
  Fresh parsley

Sauté Canadian bacon. Poach eggs. Split and toast English muffins. Top each muffin half with a slice of Canadian bacon. Place a poached egg on top of bacon. Spoon Hollandaise Sauce generously over egg. Garnish with orange slices and fresh parsley sprigs.

Hollandaise Sauce

6 egg yolks
1 tablespoon water
1½ teaspoons fresh lemon juice
1 cup butter
  Salt to taste

In the top of a double boiler over simmering water, place egg yolks and water. Beat until well blended and lemon-colored. Stir in lemon juice. Beat in the butter, a few pieces at a time. Beat until sauce is smooth. Stir in salt. Serve at once.

Cottage Cheese Omelet

Makes 1 serving

½ cup cottage cheese
1 tablespoon chopped chives
2 eggs
2 tablespoons water
¼ teaspoon basil
¼ teaspoon pepper
1 tablespoon butter

In a small bowl, combine cottage cheese and chives; set aside. Beat eggs with water, basil, and pepper. In an 8-inch omelet pan or skillet, heat butter until it sizzles. Pour egg mixture into skillet. Tilt pan while lifting edges of omelet so uncooked eggs can flow underneath. While top is still moist and creamy, spoon cottage cheese onto half of the omelet. Fold omelet over filling.

Eggs Benedict with Hollandaise Sauce

Asparagus Soufflé

Makes 4 servings

Grated Parmesan cheese
1 10¾-ounce can condensed cream of asparagus soup
¾ cup shredded Cheddar cheese
4 eggs, separated
¼ teaspoon grated lemon peel

Preheat oven to 350° F. Butter a 1½-quart soufflé dish; dust with grated Parmesan cheese. Wrap a 4-inch band of triple-thickness aluminum foil around the dish, overlapping 2 inches. Fasten to soufflé dish so that collar extends 2 inches above rim of dish. Lightly butter 1 side of foil band; dust with Parmesan cheese. In a saucepan over medium heat, combine soup and Cheddar cheese. Cook and stir soup mixture until cheese melts. Remove from heat; add gradually to unbeaten egg yolks. Beat until mixture is well blended. With clean beaters, beat egg whites until stiff peaks form. Fold in lemon peel. Gently fold soup mixture into egg whites. Pour into soufflé dish. Bake for 45 minutes or until soufflé is puffy and delicately browned. Carefully remove foil band. Serve immediately.

Ham and Green Pepper Soufflé

Makes 6 servings

¼ cup butter *or* margarine
¼ cup all-purpose flour
½ teaspoon salt
1 cup milk
1 cup minced cooked ham
1 small green pepper, chopped
4 eggs, separated
½ teaspoon cream of tartar

Preheat oven to 350° F. Butter and flour a 1½-quart soufflé dish or casserole. In a medium saucepan over medium heat, melt butter. Blend in flour and salt. Add milk all at once. Cook, stirring constantly, until mixture thickens and bubbles. Stir in ham and green pepper. Remove sauce from heat. Lightly beat egg yolks; add to sauce. Wash the beaters. In a large bowl, beat egg whites with cream of tartar until stiff peaks form. Pour sauce mixture over egg whites; fold together just until blended. Pour into prepared dish. For a "top hat," draw a circle about 1½ inches from the edge of dish with the tip of a spoon inserted 1 inch deep. Bake for 35 minutes or until a knife inserted between the center and edge of soufflé comes out clean. Serve immediately.

Scrambled Eggs with Mushrooms

Makes 6 servings

6 eggs
¼ cup milk *or* half-and-half
1 tablespoon chopped fresh
   basil
   Salt and pepper to taste
3 tablespoons butter
2 tablespoons bacon drippings
½ pound mushrooms, sliced
4 slices bacon, crisp-cooked
   and crumbled

In a small bowl, beat together eggs, milk, basil, salt, and pepper; set aside. In a large, heavy skillet over medium heat, heat butter and 2 tablespoons bacon drippings. Add mushrooms; sauté until tender. Stir in bacon. Pour eggs over mushrooms and bacon. Cook and stir until eggs are cooked through but still moist.

Scrambled Eggs with Smoked Salmon

Makes 6 servings

5 tablespoons butter *or*
   margarine
1 onion, thinly sliced
1 green pepper, thinly
   sliced
¼ pound smoked salmon, flaked
6 eggs
¼ cup milk *or* half-and-half
   Salt and white pepper to taste
   Parsley

In a large, heavy skillet over medium heat, melt butter. Add onion and pepper; sauté until vegetables are tender. Stir in smoked salmon; sauté briefly. In a bowl, beat eggs with milk until blended. Pour eggs over salmon mixture. Cook and stir until eggs are cooked through but still moist. Season with salt and pepper. Sprinkle with parsley.

Mushroom Quiche

Makes 6 servings

2 tablespoons butter *or*
   margarine
½ pound mushrooms, sliced
¼ cup sliced green onions
1 baked 9-inch pie shell
1 cup shredded Swiss cheese
4 eggs
1 cup half-and-half *or* milk
¼ cup grated Parmesan cheese
½ teaspoon salt
½ teaspoon dry mustard
¼ teaspoon white pepper

Preheat oven to 375° F. In a large skillet over medium heat, melt butter. Add mushrooms and onions; sauté until mushrooms are tender. Arrange mushrooms and onions evenly in pie shell. Sprinkle with Swiss cheese. In a mixing bowl, beat together remaining ingredients until well blended. Pour into pie shell. Bake until a knife inserted near the center comes out clean, about 35 minutes. Let quiche stand 5 minutes before serving.

Fruit Omelet

Makes 2 omelets

½ cup flaked coconut
1 banana, sliced
4 eggs
½ cup water
½ teaspoon salt
¼ teaspoon white pepper
3 tablespoons butter

Gently mix flaked coconut with banana; set aside. In a mixing bowl, beat together eggs, water, salt, and pepper. Heat half of the butter in a 10-inch omelet pan or skillet until butter sizzles. Pour in half of the egg mixture. Tilt pan while lifting edges of omelet with a spatula so that uncooked egg flows to the bottom of the pan. While top of omelet is still moist and creamy, spread ¼ cup of the banana filling on half of the omelet. With a pancake turner, fold omelet over filling. Top with ¼ cup of the filling. Sprinkle with powdered sugar. Repeat with remaining ingredients.

Crustless Carrot Quiche

Makes 6 servings

2 cups finely shredded carrots
6 eggs
1¼ cups milk
1 tablespoon instant minced
 onion
½ teaspoon salt
¼ teaspoon ground ginger
⅛ teaspoon white pepper
1 cup shredded Cheddar cheese

Preheat oven to 350° F. Butter a 9-inch quiche pan. Place carrots in a saucepan with just enough water to cover. Simmer, covered, until carrots are tender, about 5 minutes. Drain thoroughly. In a separate bowl, beat eggs with milk, onion, salt, ginger, and pepper. Stir in carrots and cheese. Pour batter into prepared pan. Place pan in a shallow pan of hot water. Bake for about 35 minutes or until a knife inserted near the center comes out clean. Let quiche stand for 5 minutes before serving.

Classic Quiche Lorraine

Makes 6 servings

8 slices bacon, crisp-cooked
 and crumbled
1 cup shredded Swiss cheese
1 baked 9-inch pie shell
6 eggs
1¼ cups half-and-half or milk
½ teaspoon salt
¼ teaspoon nutmeg
¼ teaspoon white pepper

Preheat oven to 375° F. Sprinkle bacon and cheese into pie shell. In a mixing bowl, beat together eggs, half-and-half, and seasonings until well blended. Pour over bacon and cheese. Bake for about 40 minutes or until a knife inserted near the center comes out clean. Let stand 5 minutes before serving.

Classic Quiche Lorraine
Zucchini Frittata, 20

Zucchini Frittata

Makes 4 servings

8 eggs
½ teaspoon seasoned salt
¼ teaspoon white pepper
4 tablespoons butter *or* margarine
3 cups zucchini coins, cut in fourths
½ cup finely chopped onion
⅓ cup grated Parmesan cheese Parsley

In a medium bowl, beat eggs with salt and pepper; set aside. In a large skillet over medium heat, melt 3 tablespoons of the butter. Add zucchini and onion; sauté until vegetables are tender but not brown. Remove from skillet; set aside, covering to keep warm. In same skillet, melt remaining tablespoon butter. Pour eggs into skillet. Tilt pan while lifting edges of the omelet with a spatula so uncooked eggs can flow to bottom of pan. Cook over medium heat until bottom is golden and eggs are partially set, about 5 to 7 minutes. Sprinkle cheese over eggs. Top with zucchini-onion mixture. Cover and cook 3 minutes more. Garnish with parsley. Serve in wedges.

Goldenrod Eggs

Makes 6 servings

6 hard-boiled eggs
5 tablespoons butter
4 tablespoons all-purpose flour
½ teaspoon salt
¼ teaspoon white pepper
2 cups milk
6 slices bread

Separate whites and yolks of eggs; set aside. In a saucepan over low heat, melt butter. Stir in flour, salt, and pepper. Gradually blend in milk. Cook over medium heat, stirring constantly, until mixture thickens. Slice egg whites into sauce. Toast bread and place on individual serving dishes. Pour sauce over toast. Crumble egg yolks on top of each serving.

Deviled Eggs with Anchovies

Makes 6 servings

6 hard-boiled eggs
⅓ cup mayonnaise
4 tablespoons chopped fresh parsley
1 teaspoon anchovy paste
½ teaspoon salt
½ teaspoon cayenne
1 2½-ounce can anchovy fillets

Cut eggs in half lengthwise. Place yolks in a mixing bowl. Add mayonnaise, parsley, anchovy paste, salt, and cayenne; blend well. Mound mixture into egg whites. Place 1 anchovy fillet over each deviled egg. Refrigerate until ready to serve.

California Omelet

Makes 1 serving

7 fresh snow peas
½ red bell pepper, thinly sliced
1 tablespoon butter
3 ounces small raw shrimp, peeled and deveined
3 eggs, lightly beaten
1 teaspoon parsley
Salt and pepper to taste
Dill sprigs

In a small saucepan, bring 1 cup salted water to a boil. Add snow peas; boil 1 minute. Add red pepper; boil 2 more minutes. Drain and immediately rinse with cold water; set aside. In a 6-inch skillet over medium heat, melt butter. Add shrimp; sauté until shrimp are opaque, about 4 minutes. Add beaten eggs. Cook, stirring constantly, until eggs just begin to set. Add snow peas, pepper, and parsley; cook and stir until eggs are almost set. Cook without stirring for 1 minute more or until bottom is set. Season to taste; garnish with dill sprigs.

Mushroom Filled Puffy Omelet

Makes 2 servings

4 eggs, separated
¼ cup water
½ teaspoon cream of tartar *or* lemon juice
¼ teaspoon salt
1 tablespoon butter
Sour cream

Preheat oven to 350° F. In a large mixing bowl, beat egg whites with water and cream of tartar just until stiff peaks form. In a small bowl, beat egg yolks with salt until thick and lemon-colored. Gently fold yolks into whites until thoroughly blended. In a 10-inch omelet pan or skillet with an ovenproof handle, heat butter over medium heat until it sizzles. Add eggs; gently smooth surface. Cook until puffed and lightly browned on bottom, about 5 minutes. Bake for 10 minutes or until a knife inserted near the center comes out clean. Loosen edges with a spatula. With a sharp knife, leaving bottom of omelet intact, cut along the diameter of omelet. Spoon filling over half of the omelet. Fold omelet over filling. Garnish filled omelet with a dollop of sour cream.

Mushroom and Sour Cream Filling

1 tablespoon butter
½ cup sliced fresh mushrooms
¼ cup sour cream
¼ teaspoon dillweed

In a medium skillet over medium heat, melt butter. Add mushrooms; sauté until tender. Stir in sour cream and dillweed. Spoon into omelet.

PANCAKES & CRÊPES

Blueberry Pancakes

Makes 6 servings

2 cups all-purpose flour
1 tablespoon sugar
3 teaspoons baking powder
½ teaspoon baking soda
¼ teaspoon salt
2½ cups milk
2 eggs
2 cups blueberries
Blueberry syrup *or*
maple syrup

In a mixing bowl, stir together flour, sugar, baking powder, soda, and salt. In a separate bowl, beat milk with eggs until well blended. Add to dry ingredients all at once; stir just until dry ingredients are moistened. Stir in blueberries. Set batter aside for 30 minutes before using. Lightly butter a pancake griddle. Ladle batter, about ¼ cup for each pancake, onto hot griddle. Bake until bubbles form on top and edges are dry. Turn and bake until pancakes are cooked through. Serve with blueberry or maple syrup.

Scandinavian Pancakes

Makes 6 servings

1 cup all-purpose flour
1 teaspoon sugar
2 teaspoons grated orange peel
4 egg yolks
2 cups milk
4 tablespoons sour cream
4 egg whites
Lingonberry sauce *or*
raspberry sauce

In a mixing bowl, stir together flour, sugar, and orange peel. In a separate bowl, beat together egg yolks, milk, and sour cream. Add milk mixture to dry ingredients; blend until batter is smooth. In a small, deep bowl, beat egg whites until stiff peaks form. Fold egg whites into batter. Generously butter a large, heavy skillet. Drop batter by tablespoonfuls into hot skillet; bake until lightly browned. Turn pancake and lightly brown the other side. Serve with lingonberry sauce.

Seafood Crêpes with Mornay Sauce ___

Makes 16 crepes

4 tablespoons butter *or*
    margarine
1 medium onion, chopped
½ pound mushrooms, sliced
2 cups cooked seafood: scallops,
    shrimp *or* crab
    Mornay Sauce
½ cup grated Parmesan cheese
2 tablespoons minced fresh
    parsley
½ teaspoon salt
¼ teaspoon white pepper
16 Luncheon Crepes (this page)

Preheat oven to 375° F. Butter a large, shallow baking dish. In a large skillet over medium heat, melt butter. Add onion and mushrooms; sauté until vegetables are tender. Stir in seafood. Blend in ¾ cup of the Mornay Sauce, ¼ cup of the Parmesan cheese, parsley, salt, and pepper. Spoon about 2 tablespoons of the filling down the center of unbrowned side of each crepe. Roll up and place seam side down in casserole. Repeat with remaining crepes. Top with remaining sauce and Parmesan cheese. Bake for 15 minutes.

Mornay Sauce

3 tablespoons butter *or*
    margarine
3 tablespoons all-purpose flour
2 cups milk
2 tablespoons dry white wine
2 tablespoons grated Swiss
    cheese
    Salt and pepper to taste
1 egg yolk mixed with
    ½ cup half-and-half

In a small saucepan over medium heat, melt butter. Blend in flour. Stir in milk. Cook, stirring constantly, until sauce thickens. Add wine and cheese; blend well. Season with salt and pepper. Remove from heat. Add egg yolk mixture, blend well.

Luncheon Crêpes _____

Makes 16 crepes

1 cup milk
½ cup water
2 eggs
2 tablespoons butter, melted
2 tablespoons vegetable oil
1 cup all-purpose flour
¼ teaspoon salt

In a mixing bowl, combine all ingredients; blend until smooth. Cover batter; set aside at room temperature for 30 minutes. Butter or oil a crepe pan. Heat pan until butter sizzles or oil is hot. Add 2 tablespoons of the batter. Immediately tilt pan from side to side so that batter covers the bottom of the pan. Cook about 1½ minutes or until crepe is lightly browned on one side. Turn out onto a paper towel. Repeat with remaining batter.

Crepes freeze well. To freeze, stack crepes, separating them with layers of waxed paper. Wrap stack in a moisture-proof bag. Thaw one hour before using.

Manicotti Crêpes

Makes about 18 crepes

¼ cup olive oil *or* salad oil
1 large onion, thinly sliced
2 cloves garlic, minced
1 2-pound can Italian
    tomatoes
1 6-ounce can tomato paste
1½ cups water
1 teaspoon honey
2 tablespoons minced fresh
    parsley
1 teaspoon basil
1 teaspoon oregano
    Salt and pepper to taste
2 pounds ricotta cheese
½ pound mozzarella cheese,
    shredded
¼ cup grated Parmesan cheese
2 eggs
1 tablespoon minced fresh
    parsley
    Salt and pepper to taste
16 Luncheon Crepes (page 24)
2 tablespoons grated Parmesan
    cheese

In a large saucepan over medium heat, heat oil. Add onion and garlic; sauté until onion is tender. Stir in tomatoes, tomato paste, water, honey, parsley, basil, oregano, salt, and pepper. Bring mixture to a boil. Reduce heat to simmer and continue cooking, stirring occasionally, for 45 minutes.

Preheat oven to 350° F. In a large mixing bowl, stir together cheeses, eggs, parsley, salt, and pepper until well mixed. Spoon a thin layer of sauce over the bottom of a 9 x 13-inch casserole. Spoon about 2 tablespoons of the cheese mixture along the center of each crepe; roll up. Arrange in casserole seam side down. Cover generously with sauce. (Reserve unused sauce for use in other Italian dishes.) Sprinkle with 2 tablespoons Parmesan cheese. Bake, uncovered, for 15 minutes or until heated through.

Potato Pancakes with Sour Cream

Makes 6 to 8 servings

4 medium potatoes, peeled
    and grated
1 onion, grated
1 egg, lightly beaten
½ teaspoon salt
½ teaspoon baking soda
4 to 6 tablespoons butter
2 cups sour cream

Press potatoes with a paper towel to remove as much liquid as possible. In a large mixing bowl, stir together potato, onion, and egg until well mixed. Blend in salt and soda. In a large, heavy skillet, heat 1 tablespoon of the butter until it sizzles. Drop batter by heaping tablespoonfuls into skillet. Cook until golden brown on one side. Turn; continue cooking until pancakes are cooked through, adding butter as needed. Serve hot with sour cream.

Chocolate Chip Buttermilk Pancakes

Makes 4 servings

1 cup sifted all-purpose flour
¾ teaspoon baking soda
¼ teaspoon salt
1 egg, lightly beaten
1 cup buttermilk
2 tablespoons melted butter
1 cup semisweet chocolate chips

In a mixing bowl, stir together flour, soda, and salt. In a separate bowl, beat egg with buttermilk and melted butter until well blended. Add buttermilk mixture all at once to dry ingredients; stir just until dry ingredients are moistened. Stir in chocolate chips. Cover batter and set aside at room temperature for 20 minutes. Lightly butter a pancake griddle. Drop batter, about 1 tablespoon for each pancake, onto hot griddle. Bake pancakes until bubbles form on top and edges are dry. Turn and bake until pancakes are cooked through.

Orange Crêpes

Makes 6 to 8 servings

1¼ cups all-purpose flour
1 tablespoon sugar
¼ teaspoon salt
3 eggs, lightly beaten
1 cup milk
¾ cup water
2 tablespoons Grand Marnier, brandy, *or* orange marmalade
3 tablespoons butter, melted

In a large mixing bowl, stir together flour, sugar, and salt. Add eggs, milk, water, Grand Marnier, and melted butter; stir until blended. Set aside for 30 minutes or store in the refrigerator for several hours. Just before using, bring batter to the consistency of heavy cream by blending in water, 2 tablespoons at a time, if needed. Generously butter a 5 or 6-inch crepe pan. Heat pan until butter sizzles. Ladle about ¼ cup of the batter into pan while tilting the pan so that batter covers the bottom. When batter sets, turn crepe and lightly brown the other side. Turn out onto a paper towel. Repeat with remaining batter, adding butter as necessary.

Orange Butter

½ cup butter
½ cup powdered sugar
3 tablespoons grated orange peel
2 teaspoons lemon juice
2 tablespoons Grand Marnier *or* brandy

In a mixing bowl, blend butter, sugar, orange peel, lemon juice, and Grand Marnier. Butter each crepe with this mixture. Fold crepes into quarters. In a large, buttered skillet over low heat, warm crepes to serving temperature. Sprinkle with powdered sugar.

Chicken Crêpes with Sour Cream_____

Makes 16 crepes

4 tablespoons butter *or*
  margarine
1 onion, chopped
½ cup chopped celery
3 cups diced cooked chicken
1 cup sour cream
½ teaspoon tarragon
  Salt and pepper to taste
16 Luncheon Crepes (page 24)
  Sour cream
  Parsley sprigs

Preheat oven to 375° F. Grease a large, shallow baking dish. In a large, heavy skillet, heat butter. Add onion and celery; sauté over medium heat until vegetables are tender. Stir in chicken, sour cream, tarragon, salt, and pepper. Spoon about 2 tablespoons of the filling down the center of unbrowned side of each crepe. Roll up and place in baking dish seam side down. Repeat with remaining crepes. Top with dollops of sour cream. Bake for 15 minutes or until crepes are heated through. Garnish with parsley sprigs and more sour cream.

Basic Blintzes_____

Makes 18 blintzes

4 eggs
1¼ cups all-purpose flour
¼ teaspoon salt
1 cup milk mixed with ½ cup
  water
1 teaspoon vanilla
  Butter at room temperature

In a large bowl, beat eggs until lemon-colored. Stir together flour and salt; add to eggs alternately with milk; blend well. Set aside at room temperature for 20 minutes. In an 8-inch skillet, heat ½ teaspoon butter. Add about 2 tablespoons of the batter. Immediately tilt pan from side to side so that batter covers the bottom of the pan. Cook until lightly browned on one side. Turn out onto a paper towel. Repeat with remaining batter.

Pineapple Blintzes_____

Makes about 18 blintzes

16 ounces cream cheese
16 ounces dry cottage cheese
¾ cup sugar
1 egg
2 teaspoons grated orange peel
1 teaspoon vanilla
½ cup drained crushed
  pineapple
5 tablespoons butter *or*
  margarine
18 Basic Blintzes (this page)
  Sour cream

In a mixing bowl, combine cream cheese and cottage cheese; blend well. Stir in remaining ingredients, except butter, blintzes and sour cream. Spoon about 2 tablespoons of the filling along one "side" of each blintze. Fold over edges to form a rectangle. Roll up. In a large, heavy skillet, heat butter until it sizzles. Fry blintzes, turning once, until lightly browned on both sides. Serve hot with sour cream.

PASTA

Beet Pasta with Basil Sauce

Makes 4 servings

½ cup all-purpose flour
½ cup quick-mixing flour
2 tablespoons pureed canned beets *or* baby-food beets
½ teaspoon salt
2 eggs
2 teaspoons olive oil

2 tablespoons cider vinegar
2 tablespoons vegetable oil

In a food processor, combine flours, beets, and salt until well blended. Add eggs and olive oil; blend well. Wrap dough in aluminum foil and allow to rest at room temperature for 30 minutes. Knead dough lightly on a floured surface for 1 minute. Divide dough into quarters. Roll each quarter through a pasta machine using wide noodle cutters, keeping unused dough wrapped in aluminum foil. Place noodles on a pasta holder to dry, about 30 minutes.

Bring 4 quarts water to a boil. Add vinegar and vegetable oil. Add noodles and cook just until tender, about 1 minute. Drain noodles and transfer to a heated serving platter. Drizzle Basil Sauce over noodles; toss. Serve immediately.

Basil Sauce

6 tablespoons butter
2 tablespoons basil
½ teaspoon salt
½ teaspoon pepper

Melt butter in small saucepan. Stir in basil, salt, and pepper. Cook over low heat 3 minutes. Keep warm while cooking pasta.

Pesto Sauce

Makes 6 servings

1 cup fresh basil leaves
4 cloves garlic, minced
¼ cup pine nuts
¼ cup olive oil
½ cup grated Parmesan cheese
½ teaspoon salt

In a blender or a food processor, puree all ingredients until the consistency of a thick puree. Drizzle room temperature sauce over piping hot cooked pasta.

Seafood Fettuccine

Makes 8 servings

1 12-ounce package fettuccine
¾ pound butter
6 cloves garlic, minced
1 large onion, chopped
1 pound shrimp, peeled and deveined
1 pound bay scallops
½ cup chopped fresh parsley
¼ cup chopped fresh basil
Salt and red pepper flakes to taste

Cook fettuccine according to package directions; drain. In a large, heavy skillet, melt butter. Add garlic and onion; sauté until onion is tender. Add shrimp and bay scallops; sauté about 5 minutes. Season with parsley, basil, salt, and red pepper. Place hot fettuccine in a serving dish. Add seafood. Toss gently to mix. Serve immediately.

Pasta with Goat Cheese

Makes 8 servings

1 16-ounce package thin pasta
5 tablespoons butter
2 large red bell peppers, thinly sliced
1 medium red onion, thinly sliced
1½ cups light cream
1 tablespoon basil
6 ounces shredded goat cheese
1 cup chopped pecans

Cook pasta according to package directions; drain. In a heavy skillet over medium heat, heat 2 tablespoons of the butter. Add peppers and onion; sauté until vegetables are tender, about 3 minutes. Transfer vegetables to a mixing bowl. In a small saucepan, heat cream to just below a simmer. Add hot cream to vegetables along with basil and goat cheese. Toss gently. Transfer hot pasta to a serving bowl. Add remaining butter, vegetable-cheese mixture, and pecans; toss to mix. Serve immediately.

Easy Macaroni Egg Bake

Makes 6 servings

1 7¼-ounce package macaroni and cheese dinner
¾ cup milk
2 eggs
1 small onion, chopped
½ teaspoon salt
¼ teaspoon white pepper
6 hard-boiled eggs, chopped
½ cup chopped celery
¼ cup dry bread crumbs
3 tablespoons butter, melted

Preheat oven to 350° F. Grease an 11 x 7-inch baking dish. Prepare macaroni and cheese dinner according to package directions. In a mixing bowl, beat together milk, 2 eggs, onion, salt, and pepper until blended. Add macaroni and cheese, chopped eggs, and celery; stir until well mixed. Spread evenly in prepared baking dish. Combine bread crumbs and butter. Sprinkle over casserole. Bake for 20 minutes or until hot and bubbly. Let casserole stand 3 to 5 minutes before serving.

Straw and Hay

Makes 6 servings

1 8-ounce package egg pasta
1 8-ounce package spinach pasta
½ cup unsalted butter
1½ cups heavy cream
½ teaspoon salt
½ teaspoon pepper
1¼ cups grated Parmesan cheese

Cook egg pasta and spinach pasta separately according to package directions; drain and set aside. In a large, heavy skillet over medium heat, melt butter. Stir in cream; cook, stirring constantly, until mixture thickens slightly. Season with salt and pepper. Toss egg pasta and spinach pasta together. Divide pasta among 6 deep soup bowls. Drizzle sauce over pasta. Sprinkle with Parmesan cheese.

Noodles and Almonds

Makes 6 servings

1 8-ounce package thin noodles
5 tablespoons butter
¾ cup blanched almonds
½ pound mushrooms, sliced
¼ teaspoon salt
4 tablespoons poppy seeds
½ cup bread crumbs

Cook noodles according to package directions; drain and set aside. In a large skillet over medium heat, heat butter until it sizzles. Add almonds; sauté until lightly browned. Push almonds to one side. Add mushrooms; sauté until tender. Stir in salt and poppy seeds. Add noodles; toss with almond mixture. Transfer pasta to a serving bowl. Sprinkle with bread crumbs.

Turkey Tetrazzini

Makes 6 servings

1 8-ounce package thin spaghetti
½ cup butter
1 large onion, minced
1 pound mushrooms, sliced
1½ pounds cooked turkey breast, cubed
4 tablespoons all-purpose flour
1½ cups chicken stock
Salt and pepper to taste
1 cup half-and-half

Preheat oven to 350° F. Butter a 9 x 13-inch baking dish. Cook spaghetti according to package directions; drain and set aside. In a large, heavy skillet over medium heat, heat half of the butter until it sizzles. Add onion and mushrooms; sauté until tender. Stir in turkey. In a separate saucepan over medium heat, melt remaining butter. Blend in flour. Add chicken stock, salt, and pepper. Cook, stirring constantly, until mixture thickens. Blend in half-and-half. Stir sauce into vegetables and turkey. Add spaghetti; toss to mix. Transfer to prepared baking dish. Bake for 10 minutes or until heated through.

Stuffed Giant Pasta Shells ———————

Makes 6 servings

1 8-ounce package giant pasta
   shells
3 tablespoons butter
3 tablespoons all-purpose flour
2 cups half-and-half *or* milk
½ pound Gruyere cheese,
   shredded
½ teaspoon nutmeg
½ teaspoon salt
2 egg yolks
4 tablespoons melted butter
½ cup grated Parmesan cheese

Preheat oven to 400° F. Grease a 9 x 13-inch baking dish. Cook pasta according to package directions; drain and set aside. In a saucepan over medium heat, melt butter. Stir in flour. Add half-and-half; cook, stirring constantly, until mixture thickens. Stir in Gruyere cheese, nutmeg, and salt. Cook, stirring constantly, until cheese melts. Blend in egg yolks. Fill pasta shells with cheese mixture. Place in a baking dish filling side up. Drizzle with melted butter; sprinkle with Parmesan cheese. Bake for 15 minutes or until heated through.

Pasta with Artichoke Hearts ———————

Makes 6 servings

¾ pound spaghetti
2 9-ounce packages frozen
   artichoke hearts
4 tablespoons vegetable oil
1 onion, thinly sliced
4 large tomatoes, peeled and
   chopped
½ teaspoon salt
½ teaspoon pepper
½ teaspoon garlic powder
¼ cup chopped fresh parsley

Cook spaghetti according to package directions; drain and set aside. Cook artichoke hearts according to package directions; set aside. In a large skillet, heat oil. Add onion; sauté until tender. Stir in artichoke hearts; sauté for 2 minutes. Stir in tomatoes, salt, pepper, and garlic powder. Divide spaghetti among 6 plates. Top with artichoke heart sauce; sprinkle with parsley.

Little Shells with Ham and Cheese ———

Makes 6 servings

1 8-ounce package small pasta
   shells
3 tablespoons butter at room
   temperature
1 cup ricotta cheese
1 8-ounce package cream cheese
   at room temperature
½ teaspoon tarragon
   Salt and pepper to taste
8 ounces cooked ham, shredded

Cook pasta shells according to package directions; drain and set aside. In a deep bowl, blend butter, ricotta cheese, and cream cheese. Add tarragon, salt, and pepper; beat mixture until light and fluffy. Stir in ham. Toss cheese mixture with hot pasta.

MEAT, FISH, & POULTRY

Beef Burgundy

Makes 8 servings

2 slices bacon, chopped
2 pounds beef tenderloin, cut into thin strips
1 tablespoon flour
¼ teaspoon thyme
½ cup burgundy
½ cup beef broth
¼ cup tomato paste
1 bay leaf
2 tablespoons butter
½ pound mushrooms, sliced
16 small frozen onions

In a large, heavy skillet over medium heat, sauté bacon until crisp. Add tenderloin; sprinkle with flour and thyme. Add burgundy, broth, tomato paste, and bay leaf; stir until well mixed. Reduce heat to low, cover, and simmer until almost tender, about 1½ hours.

In another skillet, melt butter; add mushrooms and onions; sauté until golden. Add to beef mixture; stir until well mixed.

Saucy Canadian Bacon

16 slices Canadian bacon
½ cup firmly packed light brown sugar
1 teaspoon dry mustard
1 tablespoon cider vinegar

Sauté Canadian bacon. Place on a serving platter. In a small saucepan, heat sugar, mustard, and vinegar over medium heat until sugar melts and sauce is hot. Drizzle sauce over bacon.

Fried Kippers

Makes 8 servings

6 tablespoons butter
1 large onion, thinly sliced
8 smoked kippers

In a large, heavy skillet, heat butter. Add onion; sauté over medium heat until tender. Add 4 kippers; fry 4 minutes on each side, turning once. Repeat with remaining kippers, adding more butter as necessary. Serve warm with onions and pan juices.

Fried Catfish

Makes 6 to 8 servings

2 pounds catfish fillets
Salt and pepper to taste
½ teaspoon garlic powder
Tabasco sauce
1 cup yellow cornmeal
3 tablespoons all-purpose flour
Vegetable oil
Tomato sauce *or* tartar sauce

Season fillets with salt, pepper, garlic powder, and Tabasco sauce. Cut fillets into 2-inch-wide strips. In a shallow bowl, stir together cornmeal and flour. Dredge fish in cornmeal mixture. Fill a heavy skillet with oil to a depth of 1 inch. Heat oil to 375° F. Fry fish, 4 pieces at a time, until cooked and golden brown. Serve with tomato sauce or tartar sauce.

Grilled Fish with Beurre Blanc Sauce

Makes 8 servings

3 tablespoons vegetable oil
1 3½-pound trout *or* salmon, cleaned, with head and tail intact
2 tablespoons wine vinegar
¼ cup white wine
1 medium onion, minced
½ cup butter

Place fish in an oiled wire broiling basket. Drizzle vegetable oil over fish. Cook on a hot grill about 5 inches from coals, turning after 5 minutes. Cook until fish flakes easily with a fork, about 10 more minutes. While fish cooks, prepare sauce. In a medium saucepan over medium heat, bring vinegar, wine, and onion to a boil. Simmer until mixture is reduced by half. Gradually blend in butter. Place fish on a serving platter; drizzle with sauce.

Barbecued Shrimp

Makes 6 servings

24 large shrimp, shelled, deveined, tails intact
1 large onion, thinly sliced
24 slices bacon
2 tablespoons brown sugar
2 tablespoons soy sauce
2 tablespoons dry sherry
3 cloves garlic, minced
½ teaspoon chili powder
½ teaspoon ground ginger
½ teaspoon salt
Shredded lettuce

Cut shrimp along inside curve and open out butterfly-style. Place an onion on one half of shrimp; fold shrimp together. Wrap a slice of bacon around shrimp; secure with a toothpick. Set aside. Repeat with remaining shrimp. In a small bowl, mix brown sugar, soy sauce, sherry, garlic, and seasonings until well blended. Dip shrimp into marinade; set aside on a barbecue rack or broiling tray for 30 minutes. Barbecue over medium fire or grill under broiler until shrimp are cooked and bacon is crisp, about 5 minutes. Serve on a bed of shredded lettuce.

Turkey Mousse

Makes 4 servings

1½ cups turkey stock *or* chicken
    stock
1 package unflavored gelatin
1½ cups minced, cooked turkey
¼ cup mayonnaise
1 small onion, minced
1 stalk celery, minced
1 teaspoon celery salt
½ teaspoon curry powder
¾ cup heavy cream, whipped
    Fresh vegetables

Lightly oil a 1-quart mold. Place ½ cup of the turkey stock in a small heatproof bowl or cup. Sprinkle gelatin over stock; let soften for about 1 minute. Set bowl in a pan of simmering water; stir constantly until gelatin dissolves. Remove from heat. In a mixing bowl, combine remaining ingredients, except heavy cream and fresh vegetables. Blend in dissolved gelatin. Refrigerate until mixture begins to set. Fold in whipped cream. Spoon mixture into mold. Cover lightly; chill overnight. When ready to serve, unmold and garnish with fresh vegetables.

Oven-Fried Chicken Nuggets

Makes 8 to 10 servings

1 cup seasoned bread crumbs
½ teaspoon garlic powder
3 chicken breasts, skinned,
    boned, and cut into 1-inch
    pieces
½ cup butter, melted

Preheat oven to 400° F. In a shallow bowl, mix bread crumbs with garlic powder. Dip chicken pieces into melted butter; roll in bread crumbs, and place on a baking sheet. Bake for 10 to 12 minutes. Serve hot with Tartar Sauce.

Tartar Sauce

1 cup mayonnaise
2 green onions, chopped
2 teaspoons capers
1 medium dill pickle, minced
1 clove garlic, minced

In a small bowl, combine all ingredients. Stir until well mixed. Place in a covered container; chill until ready to serve.

Toad-in-the-Hole

Makes 8 servings

4 eggs, beaten
½ teaspoon salt
1 cup milk
2 cups all-purpose flour, sifted
2 pounds pork sausages, cut in
    ¾-inch pieces

Preheat oven to 425° F. In a large mixing bowl, combine eggs, salt, and milk. Blend in flour. Set aside for 15 minutes. In a heavy skillet over medium-high heat, sauté sausage. Distribute drippings among eight 3-inch pie tins. Pour a thin layer (about ¼ inch) of batter into each tin. Bake for 5 minutes or until set. Add sausage; top with remaining batter. Bake for about 25 minutes or until puffed up and browned. Serve at once.

SANDWICHES

Orange Date Tea Sandwiches

Makes 6 sandwiches

1 large orange, peeled and
   segmented
1 8-ounce package cream cheese
   at room temperature
½ cup pitted chopped dates
1 16-ounce can brown bread
   Butter at room temperature

Cut orange segments into small pieces. In a mixing bowl, stir together cream cheese, dates, and orange pieces. Slice brown bread into 12 slices. Butter slices; spread 6 slices with filling. Top with remaining slices. Place sandwiches on a serving tray, cover with plastic wrap, and chill until ready to serve.

Cream Cheese Fruit Sandwiches

Makes 8 small sandwiches

1 8-ounce package cream cheese
   at room temperature
1 8-ounce can crushed
   pineapple, drained
½ teaspoon vanilla
¼ cup chopped dark red cherries
8 slices white *or* whole
   wheat bread

In a mixing bowl, stir together cream cheese, pineapple, and vanilla until well mixed. Stir in cherries. Assemble 4 sandwiches. With cookie cutters or a sharp knife, cut sandwiches into desired shapes.

Barbecued Beef on Buns

Makes 6 sandwiches

1½ pounds ground beef
  1 onion, thinly sliced
    Salt and pepper to taste
  1 cup catsup
  1 tablespoon mustard
  3 tablespoons brown sugar
  2 tablespoons red wine vinegar
  1 teaspoon Worcestershire
    sauce
  6 hamburger buns, split

In a large skillet over medium heat, sauté hamburger and onion until hamburger is browned and onion is tender. Pour off excess fat. Add remaining ingredients. Cook and stir until mixture simmers. Toast hamburger buns. Fill with meat mixture.

Broiled Monte Cristo, 40

Chicken Sandwiches Veronique ———

Makes 12 sandwiches

3½ cups cubed cooked chicken
  1 cup chopped celery
  ¾ cup seedless grapes, halved
  ½ cup chopped pecans
  ¼ cup coconut flakes
  ¾ cup mayonnaise
  ½ teaspoon curry powder
    (optional)
    Salt and pepper to taste
  ¼ cup heavy cream, whipped
12 croissants
    Lettuce leaves
    Tomato slices

In a large mixing bowl, stir together chicken, celery, grapes, pecans, and coconut. In a separate bowl, combine mayonnaise, curry powder, salt, and pepper; fold into whipped cream. Fold chicken mixture gently into whipped cream mixture. Cover and chill. Slice open croissants; line openings with lettuce leaves and tomato slices. Fill with chicken mixture.

Broiled Monte Cristo ————————

Makes 3 sandwiches

  6 slices bread
  6 slices cooked turkey
  6 slices cooked ham
  3 eggs
  2 tablespoons water
  2 tablespoons vegetable oil
  1 tablespoon butter
1½ cups shredded provolone
    cheese
  ½ cup milk
  ½ cup mayonnaise
  ⅛ teaspoon nutmeg
    Parsley
    Lemon slices

Assemble 3 sandwiches, each filled with 2 slices of the turkey and 2 slices of the ham. Beat eggs with water in a shallow bowl. In a frying pan, heat oil and butter. Dip both sides of one sandwich in eggs. Fry both sides of the sandwich until golden brown. Repeat with remaining sandwiches. Place sandwiches in a baking dish. In a saucepan, combine cheese, milk, mayonnaise, and nutmeg. Heat, stirring constantly, until cheese melts and mixture is smooth. Pour over sandwiches. Broil 6 inches from heat for 5 minutes or until bubbly. Garnish with parsley and lemon slices.

Sardine Cornucopias ———————

Makes 12 sandwiches

12 slices dark sandwich bread
  2 2¾-ounce cans sardines,
    drained
  4 hard-boiled eggs, chopped
  1 tablespoon lemon juice
    Butter

Cut crusts from bread. In a mixing bowl, combine remaining ingredients until well mixed. Spread bread slices with filling. Bring opposite corners of bread together to form a triangle. Spread edges of bread with butter; press together. Secure with a wooden pick. Cover sandwiches with a damp cloth; refrigerate at least 1 hour. Remove toothpicks before serving.

Asparagus Roll-Ups

Makes 12 sandwiches

12 slices fresh white bread,
   crusts removed
1 8-ounce package cream cheese
   at room temperature
4 tablespoons sour cream
1 10-ounce package frozen
   asparagus spears, cooked
   Melted butter
   Nutmeg

Preheat broiler. Flatten each slice of bread with a rolling pin. In a small bowl, stir together cream cheese and sour cream until well blended. Spread cheese mixture on bread. Place an asparagus spear on each slice of bread. Roll up jelly roll style. Place seam side down on a baking sheet. Brush with melted butter. Sprinkle lightly with nutmeg. Bake, turning once, until lightly browned.

Hot Roast Beef Sandwiches

Makes 8 sandwiches

¼ cup butter
1 large red onion, thinly sliced
1 pound mushrooms, sliced
½ cup dry sherry
1 bouillon cube, dissolved in ½
   cup hot water
1 teaspoon fresh lemon juice
1 teaspoon Worcestershire
   sauce
2½ pounds sirloin tip roast,
   cooked and thinly sliced
8 party rolls or pita breads

In a large, heavy skillet over medium heat, heat butter until it sizzles. Add onion; sauté until tender. Add mushrooms; sauté briefly. Stir in sherry, bouillon, lemon juice, and Worcestershire sauce; simmer 5 minutes. Push vegetables to side of pan; add sliced beef. Spoon vegetables and sauce over beef. Cover pan; simmer until beef is hot. Warm the rolls; split and fill with beef and vegetables.

Chicago Style Open-Face

Makes 6 sandwiches

6 slices rye bread
½ head iceberg lettuce, cut into
   6 portions
6 slices Swiss cheese
12 ounces sliced turkey *or*
   chicken
6 slices cooked bacon, halved
1 large tomato, cut into 6 slices

On each slice of bread, place a wedge of lettuce; top with a slice of Swiss cheese. Distribute turkey among the 6 sandwiches. Drizzle sandwiches with Zesty Dressing. Cross 2 bacon strips over each sandwich; top with a tomato slice.

Zesty Dressing

2 cups mayonnaise
4 tablespoons chili sauce
4 tablespoons chopped sweet
   pickle
1 small red onion, minced

In a deep bowl, stir together all ingredients until well mixed. Cover and chill until ready to serve.

Tuna Salad Filling _____

Makes 3 cups

2 7½-ounce cans tuna, drained
2 hard-boiled eggs, chopped
1 small red onion, thinly sliced
½ cup chopped celery
½ cup mayonnaise
½ teaspoon salt
½ teaspoon garlic powder
¼ teaspoon pepper

In a large mixing bowl, flake tuna. Add remaining ingredients; toss to mix. Cover with plastic wrap and refrigerate until ready to serve. Good on dark rolls or white toast, or as a stuffing for tomatoes.

Turkey Salad Filling _____

Makes 7 cups

2½ cups diced cooked chicken
2 cups chopped celery
¾ cup toasted almonds, chopped
   Salt and pepper to taste
½ teaspoon celery seed
½ teaspoon garlic powder
1 cup mayonnaise
1 tablespoon fresh lemon juice
1 red bell pepper, chopped

In a mixing bowl, stir together all ingredients until well blended. Adjust seasonings. Cover and chill until ready to assemble sandwiches.

Beef and Cream Cheese Filling _____

Makes 1½ cups

1 8-ounce package cream
   cheese
½ cup chopped cooked beef
1 red onion, minced
3 tablespoons half-and-half
¼ cup mayonnaise
¼ teaspoon Worcestershire
   sauce

In a mixing bowl, stir together all ingredients until well mixed. Cover and chill until ready to assemble sandwiches.

Egg and Cheese Spread _____

Makes 4 cups

6 hard-boiled eggs, chopped
¾ cup grated Cheddar cheese
¼ cup chopped pecans
1 tablespoon chopped pimiento
½ cup mayonnaise

In a mixing bowl, blend together all ingredients until mixture is of spreading consistency. Excellent for sandwiches or as a stuffing for celery stalks.

SALADS

Gazpacho Macaroni Salad _____

Makes 6 to 8 servings

2 cups uncooked macaroni
1 10-ounce package frozen peas
3 medium tomatoes, peeled and chopped
1 cup chopped celery
1 medium cucumber, diced
1 green pepper, chopped
5 green onions, thinly sliced
6 ounces salami, cubed
¼ cup chopped fresh parsley
⅓ cup olive oil
¼ cup wine vinegar
1 teaspoon salt
½ teaspoon Worcestershire sauce
   Hot pepper sauce to taste
1 clove garlic, pressed
   Lettuce cups
   Ripe olives

Cook macaroni according to package directions; drain; rinse in cold water; drain again. Place peas in a bowl; cover with boiling water; let stand 1 to 2 minutes; drain. In a bowl, combine macaroni, peas, tomatoes, celery, cucumber, green pepper, onions, salami, and parsley. In a separate bowl, beat together remaining ingredients until well blended. Pour over macaroni mixture; toss lightly. Serve in lettuce cups; garnish with olives. Note: macaroni and vegetable mixture may be combined with dressing and chilled 3 hours before serving. Toss before spooning into lettuce cups.

Special Salad _____

Makes 8 servings

½ cup olive oil
½ cup lemon juice or vinegar
¼ teaspoon dry mustard
   Salt and pepper to taste
1 romaine lettuce, torn into bite-size pieces
4 tomatoes, cut into wedges
1 green pepper, sliced
1 large red onion, sliced
½ cup chopped fresh parsley
2 hard-boiled eggs, sliced
1 2½-ounce can anchovy fillets
½ cup black olives
¼ pound feta cheese

In a small bowl, combine olive oil, lemon juice, mustard, salt, and pepper; blend well. Place lettuce, tomatoes, green pepper, onion, and parsley in a serving bowl. Add dressing to taste; toss lightly. Add eggs, anchovies, and olives; toss again. Crumble feta cheese over top of salad.

Mushroom Salad

Makes 8 servings

1 cup salad oil
4 tablespoons wine vinegar
4 tablespoons fresh lemon juice
    Salt and pepper to taste
2 teaspoons basil
1 teaspoon Dijon mustard
¼ teaspoon paprika
2 pounds medium mushrooms
2 cups cherry tomatoes
1 large onion, thinly sliced

In a large glass serving bowl, mix oil, vinegar, lemon juice, salt, and seasonings. Stir in mushrooms, tomatoes, and onion. Chill 8 hours, stirring occasionally.

Vegetable Salad

Makes 8 servings

½ small cauliflower, broken
    into flowerets
½ pound green beans
1 16-ounce can kidney beans
1 16-ounce can garbanzos
4 green onions, chopped
1 2¼-ounce can sliced olives
½ cup olive oil
¼ cup wine vinegar
1 teaspoon tarragon
    Salt and pepper to taste
1 bunch leaf lettuce
1 head Boston lettuce
3 large tomatoes, sliced
3 hard-boiled eggs, sliced

Blanch cauliflower and green beans. Drain canned beans. In a mixing bowl, toss together cauliflower, beans, onions, and olives. Chill until just before serving time. In a small bowl, combine oil, vinegar, tarragon, salt, and pepper. Pour over chilled vegetables; toss. Tear lettuce into bite-sized pieces; arrange on a platter. Arrange vegetables over lettuce. Arrange tomato slices and hard-boiled eggs attractively on top.

Potato Salad

Makes 8 servings

2 pounds small red potatoes,
    cooked and drained
5 tablespoons vegetable oil
3 tablespoons red wine vinegar
2 cloves garlic, minced
    Salt and pepper to taste
1 pound Italian sausage,
    cooked and sliced into ¾-inch
    pieces
1 onion, thinly sliced
1 red bell pepper, sliced

Slice potatoes and place in a serving bowl. Add oil, vinegar, minced garlic, salt, and pepper; toss gently to coat potatoes. Stir in sausage, onion, and red pepper. Chill until ready to serve.

Salad Nicoise

Makes 6 to 8 servings

1 head Boston lettuce
¾ pound new potatoes, boiled, peeled, and sliced
¾ pound green beans, trimmed, cooked, and drained
4 hard-boiled eggs, sliced
1 large Bermuda onion, sliced
3 large tomatoes, sliced
2 green peppers, sliced
1 2-ounce can anchovy fillets, drained
2 7-ounce cans solid-pack tuna
1 cup pitted ripe olives

Tear lettuce into bite-size pieces; arrange on a serving platter. Arrange remaining ingredients attractively over lettuce. Drizzle Basil Vinaigrette over salad. Chill until ready to serve.

Basil Vinaigrette

½ cup corn oil *or* olive oil
¼ cup red wine vinegar
2 cloves garlic, minced
2 teaspoons basil
½ teaspoon salt
¼ teaspoon freshly ground black pepper

In a jar with a tight-fitting lid, combine all ingredients. Shake until blended.

Orange Tailgate Salad

Makes 8 to 10 servings

1 bunch leaf lettuce
6 large oranges, peeled and sliced
2 bananas, sliced
1 avocado, sliced
1 pint strawberries
3 peaches, cut into chunks

Arrange lettuce leaves on a flat platter. Arrange fruit over lettuce.

Yogurt Dressing

1 cup plain yogurt
2 teaspoons lime juice
Honey to taste
Dash salt
Lime slices

In a small bowl, combine all ingredients except lime slices. Line a serving bowl with lime slices. Spoon in yogurt.

Fruits

Berry Swirl Delight

Makes 6 servings

2 pints strawberries, hulled
  and sliced
1 pint blueberries
¾ cup sugar
¼ cup fresh orange juice
3 tablespoons orange liqueur *or*
  Triple Sec to taste
1 cup heavy cream

In a serving dish, combine strawberries and blueberries. Sprinkle with ½ cup of the sugar, orange juice, and liqueur. Toss fruit gently. In a separate bowl, whip cream until soft peaks form. Gradually add remaining sugar; continue beating until stiff peaks form and sugar dissolves. Swirl cream into berries for a marbled effect.

Fruit Whip with Custard Sauce

Makes 6 servings

1 envelope unflavored gelatin
½ cup boiling water
2 tablespoons fresh lemon juice
1 12-ounce package frozen fruit
  of your choice
5 egg whites

In a blender container, combine gelatin, water, and lemon juice. Cover and blend at medium speed until gelatin dissolves, about 45 seconds. Separate pieces of frozen fruit by rapping the package sharply against counter edge. Place half of the fruit in blender with gelatin mixture. Blend at medium speed for 10 seconds. Add remaining fruit; blend just until smooth. Beat egg whites until stiff peaks form. Fold fruit into egg whites. Spoon into serving dishes; chill for 3 hours. Serve with Custard Sauce.

Custard Sauce

4 egg yolks
¼ cup sugar
⅛ teaspoon salt
1¼ cups milk
½ teaspoon rum extract

In a small, heavy saucepan, beat egg yolks lightly. Add sugar and salt; mix until well blended. Gradually stir in milk. Cook over low heat, stirring constantly, until mixture thickens and coats a metal spoon. Stir in rum extract. Cool to room temperature. Cover with plastic wrap; chill thoroughly.

Strawberry Soup

Makes 6 to 8 servings

1½ cups water
1 cup dry red wine
½ cup sugar
Freshly squeezed juice of 2 lemons
½ teaspoon cinnamon
¼ teaspoon nutmeg
1 quart strawberries, hulled and pureed
1 cup heavy cream, whipped
¼ cup sour cream
Fresh strawberries, sliced

In a medium saucepan, combine water, wine, sugar, lemon juice, cinnamon, and nutmeg. Over medium heat, bring mixture, uncovered, to a boil. Reduce heat; simmer for 10 minutes, stirring occasionally. Add strawberry puree; simmer 10 minutes, stirring often. Cool at room temperature, then cover and refrigerate until well chilled. Just before serving, combine heavy cream and sour cream in a small bowl. Add to strawberry mixture; blend well. Garnish with sliced strawberries.

Fruit Soup

Makes 8 to 10 servings

1 cup pitted prunes
1 cup raisins
1 cup dried apples
2 quarts water
2 tablespoons fresh lemon juice
1 teaspoon grated lemon peel
2 small sticks cinnamon
½ cup dark corn syrup
¼ cup instant tapioca

In a large saucepan, combine prunes, raisins, dried apples, and water. Set aside 8 hours or overnight. Stir in remaining ingredients. Bring mixture to a boil over medium heat. Reduce heat; simmer 1 hour. Discard cinnamon sticks before serving. Serve hot or chilled.

Cherry Soup

Makes 8 servings

3 16-ounce cans pitted tart cherries, drained, juice reserved
1 cup water
¼ cup sugar
½ teaspoon cinnamon
½ teaspoon allspice
¼ teaspoon nutmeg
1 cup dry red wine
1 pint heavy cream or half-and-half

Chop cherries and place in a medium saucepan. Stir in water, sugar, cinnamon, allspice, and nutmeg. Bring mixture to a boil over medium heat. Reduce heat; simmer, covered, for 4 minutes. Ladle mixture into a tureen. Stir in red wine and cream. Cover with plastic wrap and chill until ready to serve.

Pink Grapefruit Ice

Makes 4 servings

3 medium pink grapefruit,
   peeled, segmented,
   membranes removed
⅔ cup sugar
¼ cup water
3 tablespoons rum
1 cup fresh blackberries

In a food processor, process grapefruit, sugar, water, and rum until very smooth. Pour mixture into a 9 x 13-inch pan. Freeze at least 4 hours. Return mixture to processor; process until very smooth and light. Freeze again until just firm, about 45 minutes. Set aside to soften at room temperature for 10 minutes. Spoon into serving dishes; garnish with blackberries.

Fresh Fruit Compote

Makes 8 servings

½ cup water
1 cup sugar
1 cup dry white wine
½ cup white creme de
   menthe
1 cup fresh orange juice
¼ cup fresh lemon juice
1 pint strawberries
1 pint blueberries
4 cups peeled, sliced fresh
   peaches
1½ cups sour cream
½ teaspoon nutmeg
   Mint sprigs

In a saucepan, combine water and sugar; bring to a boil over medium heat. Reduce heat; simmer for 5 minutes, stirring occasionally. Pour into a large glass bowl. Add wine, creme de menthe, orange juice, and lemon juice; blend well. Stir in fruits. Place in refrigerator to marinate 8 hours or overnight. Divide fruits and marinade among 8 sherbet glasses. Garnish with sour cream, nutmeg, and sprigs of mint.

Yogurt Peach Ambrosia

Makes 8 servings

2 cups sliced peaches
2 bananas, sliced
3 oranges, peeled and thinly
   sliced
1 tablespoon fresh lemon
   juice
1 cup coconut
1 cup miniature marshmallows
1 cup unflavored yogurt *or*
   lemon flavored yogurt
   Mint leaves, optional

In a serving bowl, combine fruit and lemon juice. Toss lightly; drain excess juice. Chill for 1 hour. Stir in coconut, marshmallows, and yogurt. Serve in sherbet glasses; garnish with fresh mint leaves, if available.

Yogurt Peach Ambrosia

VEGETABLES

Baked Zucchini

Makes 6 servings

6 medium zucchini, cut into
rounds
Butter
Salt and pepper to taste
Grated Parmesan cheese

Preheat oven to 375° F. Grease a shallow, 2-quart baking dish. Arrange zucchini in prepared baking dish. Dot zucchini with butter; sprinkle with salt, pepper, and Parmesan cheese. Bake until tender, about 10 minutes.

Sweet Sour Red Cabbage

Makes 8 servings

5 tablespoons bacon drippings
2 onions, sliced
2 small heads red cabbage,
shredded
4 tart apples, sliced
¾ cup cider vinegar
1 cup packed brown sugar
½ teaspoon cloves
2 bay leaves
Dash pepper
¼ teaspoon allspice
2 cups cranberry juice

In a large skillet, heat bacon drippings. Add onions; sauté until tender. Transfer onions and drippings to a large, heavy pot. Stir in remaining ingredients. Simmer, covered, until cabbage is very tender. Adjust seasonings. Discard bay leaves before serving.

Vegetables Tempura

Makes 6 to 8 servings

3 eggs
1 cup ice water
1 cup all-purpose flour
½ teaspoon baking powder
Peanut oil
1 medium sweet potato, peeled
and cut into ¼-inch slices
2 carrots, cut into ¼-inch strips
2 green peppers, cut into
¼-inch strips
1 small eggplant, cut into
¼-inch slices

In a mixing bowl, beat eggs with ice water until light. Sift in flour and baking powder. Whisk the mixture, adding enough water to make a thin batter. Set aside for 30 minutes. In wok or heavy skillet, heat oil to 375° F. Piece by piece, dip vegetables first into batter, then slide into hot oil. Fry ingredients of the same kind together, but do not overcrowd the wok. Drain on paper toweling. Serve hot.

Fall Vegetable Combination _____

Makes 6 to 8 servings

2 potatoes, peeled and diced
2 rutabagas, peeled and diced
2 cups chicken stock
1 cup water
1 teaspoon salt
  Salt and pepper to taste
1 cup grated Cheddar cheese
1 medium onion, chopped

In a large saucepan, combine all ingredients except cheese and onion. Cook, covered, over medium heat until vegetables are tender. Drain vegetables; mash thoroughly or puree. Stir in cheese and onion until well mixed. Serve hot.

Ratatouille _____

Makes 8 servings

1 large eggplant, peeled and cut into 1-inch cubes
  Salt
¼ cup olive oil
1 large onion, thinly sliced
3 cloves garlic, minced
2 medium zucchini, cut into ½-inch slices
3 large tomatoes, peeled and diced
1 green pepper, chopped
1 teaspoon basil
  Salt and pepper to taste
½ teaspoon oregano

Sprinkle eggplant with salt; set aside for 15 minutes. Rinse, then press out excess moisture. In a large saucepan over medium heat, heat olive oil. Add onion and garlic; sauté until tender. Stir in remaining ingredients; cook, covered, for 15 minutes. Uncover and continue cooking, stirring occasionally, until vegetables are tender, about 10 more minutes.

Vermont Baked Beans _____

Makes 8 servings

1 pound dried pea beans
8 cups water
5 slices bacon, cut into 1-inch pieces
1 large onion, thinly sliced
½ cup maple syrup
¼ cup dark rum
3 tablespoons brown sugar
3 tablespoons butter, melted
1 teaspoon salt

Place beans in a medium saucepan with 8 cups water. Bring beans to a boil over medium heat. Continue boiling for 2 minutes. Remove beans from heat and let stand at room temperature for 1 hour. Return to a boil, then reduce heat to a simmer and continue cooking for about 40 minutes. Drain beans, reserving 2½ cups liquid. In a bean-pot or heavy casserole dish, stir together beans, bacon, and onion. In a small bowl, blend maple syrup, rum, brown sugar, butter, and salt. Pour over beans and bacon. Add reserved cooking liquid. Stir mixture thoroughly. Cover and bake in a 325° oven for 3½ hours.

Eggplant Parmigiana

Makes 6 servings

1 cup olive oil
1 large eggplant *or* two small
   eggplants, peeled and cut into
   ½-inch slices
1¼ cups Tomato Sauce
6 tablespoons grated Parmesan
   cheese
½ pound mozzarella cheese,
   thinly sliced

Preheat oven to 400° F. In a large, heavy skillet, heat oil. Fry eggplant in hot oil until lightly browned; drain. In a flat casserole, arrange 1 layer of the fried eggplant. Cover with Tomato Sauce. Sprinkle with Parmesan cheese; top with a layer of mozzarella. Repeat procedure until all the eggplant is used, ending with a layer of mozzarella. Bake for 15 minutes. Serve hot.

Tomato Sauce

Makes 2½ quarts

3 tablespoons olive oil
½ stalk celery, finely chopped
1 onion, chopped
1 teaspoon minced fresh
   parsley
1 clove garlic, minced
1 28-ounce can Italian tomatoes
1 6-ounce can tomato puree
2 bay leaves
½ teaspoon salt
½ teaspoon basil
½ teaspoon pepper
½ teaspoon oregano

In a medium saucepan over medium heat, heat oil. Add celery, onion, parsley, and garlic; sauté until vegetables are tender, stirring often. Add tomatoes and tomato puree. Stir in seasonings. Simmer gently, uncovered, for 40 minutes, stirring occasionally. Remove bay leaves before serving.

Tomatoes Florentine

Makes 8 servings

8 medium tomatoes
   Salt
2 tablespoons all-purpose flour
½ teaspoon salt
¼ cup milk
1 egg yolk, lightly beaten
1 tablespoon butter, melted
1 10-ounce package frozen
   chopped spinach, cooked and
   drained

Preheat oven to 375° F. Cut a slice from the top of each tomato. Scoop out pulp, leaving a shell at least ¼ inch thick. Place tomatoes upside down on paper toweling to drain. Sprinkle the inside of each tomato with salt. In a saucepan, combine flour and salt. Blend in milk. Stir in egg yolk and melted butter. Add well-drained spinach; blend well. Cook over medium heat until spinach begins to simmer. Spoon mixture into tomatoes, mounding to form a rounded top. Arrange in a shallow baking dish. Bake for 10-15 minutes until tomatoes are cooked but not mushy. Serve hot.

Corn Pudding

Makes 6 servings

3 eggs, lightly beaten
2 cups canned corn,
  well drained
2 cups milk, scalded
1 small onion, minced
1 tablespoon butter, melted
1 teaspoon sugar
  Salt and pepper to taste

Preheat oven to 350° F. Grease a 1-quart casserole. In a deep mixing bowl, combine all ingredients. Pour mixture into prepared casserole. Set casserole in a shallow baking pan; fill pan with hot water to a depth of 1 inch. Bake until a knife inserted near the center of casserole comes out clean. Let stand 10 minutes at room temperature before serving.

Tangy Italian Green Beans

Makes 6 servings

2 9-ounce packages frozen
  Italian green beans
4 teaspoons butter
4 slices lean bacon, diced
1 small onion, minced
  Salt and pepper to taste
3 tablespoons chicken
  stock

Quickly thaw green beans by immersing them in boiling water; separate quickly with a fork. Drain well. In a saucepan over low heat, melt butter. Add bacon and onion; sauté until onion is tender. Add beans, salt, pepper, and stock. Bring mixture to a simmer; simmer, covered, until beans are tender, about 15 minutes.

Sauerkraut Casserole

Makes 8 servings

1 2-pound jar sauerkraut
12 slices lean bacon
1 large onion, thinly
  sliced
3 carrots, grated
3 apples, pared and
  sliced
½ teaspoon salt
½ teaspoon black pepper
6 slices baked ham
1 pound sausage, cut into
  1-inch pieces
3 tablespoons butter
1 cup beef bouillon
2 cups dry white wine

Preheat oven to 275° F. Wash sauerkraut in 3 changes of water; drain well. Arrange half of the sauerkraut in a 9 x 13-inch baking dish. Top with one layer each of bacon, onions, carrots, and apples. Sprinkle with salt and pepper. Arrange ham and sausage over the top; dot with butter. Cover with remaining sauerkraut. Pour bouillon and wine over all. Bake, uncovered, for 2 hours. If, after 1½ hours, the casserole seems too dry, more bouillon may be added.

DESSERTS

English Raisin Almond Cake _____

Makes 8 servings

3/4 cup butter
3/4 cup sugar
4 eggs
2 cups all-purpose flour
1 1/4 teaspoons baking powder
1 tablespoon milk, optional
3 tablespoons ground almonds
1 cup dried currants
1 cup raisins
1/2 cup candied cherry halves
1/4 cup chopped candied orange
    peel
2 teaspoons grated lemon peel
1/2 cup blanched split almonds

Preheat oven to 350° F. Butter and flour an 8-inch cake pan. In a large mixing bowl, cream butter and sugar. Add eggs, 1 at a time, beating well after each addition. In a separate bowl, stir together flour and baking powder. Add to egg mixture; blend well. If batter seems too dry, add 1 tablespoon milk. Stir in ground almonds, currants, raisins, cherries, orange peel, and lemon peel. Spoon batter evenly into prepared pan. Arrange almonds over top of cake in a decorative pattern. Bake for 1 1/2 hours or until a wooden pick inserted near the center comes out clean. Cool 10 minutes in the pan; turn out onto a wire rack to cool completely. Wait 2 days before serving. This cake keeps well in an airtight container.

Sour Cream Coffee Cake _____

Makes 8 servings

1 cup chopped walnuts
3/4 cup sugar
1 teaspoon cinnamon
1/4 cup butter
1 cup sugar
2 eggs, lightly beaten
1 cup sour cream
1 teaspoon vanilla
2 cups all-purpose flour
1 teaspoon baking powder
1 teaspoon baking soda
1/4 teaspoon salt

Preheat oven to 350° F. Grease and flour a 9-inch springform pan. In a small bowl, combine walnuts, 3/4 cup sugar, and cinnamon; set aside. In a large bowl, cream butter and 1 cup sugar. Add eggs; beat until mixture is light and fluffy. Stir in sour cream and vanilla. In a separate bowl, stir together flour, baking powder, soda, and salt; blend into sour cream mixture. Pour half of the batter into prepared pan. Sprinkle half of the nut mixture over batter. Pour in remaining batter; sprinkle with remaining nut mixture. Bake for 35 minutes or until a wooden pick inserted near center comes out clean. Cool in pan on a rack.

Summer Fruit Pie

Makes 6 servings

¾ cup crushed graham crackers
2 tablespoons melted margarine
1 teaspoon sugar
2 tablespoons apple jelly
1 tablespoon water
½ cup grapes
½ cup blueberries
½ cup strawberries, halved
2 fresh peaches, sliced

Preheat oven to 350° F. In a bowl, stir together graham crackers, margarine, and sugar until well blended. Press crumb mixture into an 8-inch pie pan. Bake for 10 minutes. In a small saucepan, stir together jelly and water. Cook over low heat for 3 minutes. Arrange fruit over baked crust. Drizzle jelly mixture over fruit. Serve either chilled or at room temperature.

Spritz Cookies

Makes 5 to 6 dozen

1 cup butter
¾ cup sugar
2 egg yolks
1 teaspoon almond extract
2 cups all-purpose flour
¼ teaspoon salt

Preheat oven to 350° F. In a large bowl, cream butter and sugar. Blend in egg yolks and almond extract. In a separate bowl, stir together flour and salt; blend into creamed mixture. Fill a cookie press with the dough. Using a variety of discs, press onto an ungreased baking sheet. Decorate as desired. Bake for 8 to 10 minutes.

Shortbread

Makes 16 servings

2 cups butter at room temperature
1 cup sugar
4 cups all-purpose flour
1 cup semolina
Powdered sugar

Preheat oven to 300° F. In a large mixing bowl, cream butter and sugar. Add half of the flour; stir to blend. Stir in remaining flour, 1 cup at a time. Add semolina; beat until dough holds together. Turn out onto a lightly floured surface; knead for 2 minutes. Divide dough into 4 parts. Pat each part into an 8-inch pie pan, pressing dough to even the surface. Prick the entire surface with a fork. Bake on the center shelf for 1¼ hours or until just beginning to turn golden brown. Cut into wedges while still warm. Sprinkle with powdered sugar. Store shortbread in airtight containers.

Old-Fashioned Bread Pudding _____

Makes 8 servings

4½ cups crumbled stale rolls *or*
  bread
4 eggs
1½ cups sugar
2 teaspoons vanilla
1 teaspoon cinnamon
½ teaspoon nutmeg
¼ cup butter at room
  temperature
4 cups milk
½ cup golden raisins
1 teaspoon grated lemon peel

Preheat oven to 350° F. Place crumbled bread on a cookie sheet; place in oven to crisp for about 10 minutes. Transfer to a 9 x 13-inch baking dish. In a mixing bowl, beat eggs and sugar until thick and lemon-colored. Add vanilla, cinnamon, and nutmeg; stir until blended. Beat in butter and milk. Sprinkle raisins and lemon peel over bread pieces. Pour egg mixture over all. Place pudding in a pan of warm water. Bake for 50 minutes or until a knife inserted in the center comes out clean. Cool slightly. Serve with Bourbon Sauce.

Bourbon Sauce

1 cup sugar
1 cup heavy cream
2 teaspoons butter
5 tablespoons water mixed
  with 1 teaspoon all-purpose
  flour
3 tablespoons bourbon

In a small saucepan over medium heat, combine sugar, heavy cream, and butter. Bring to a boil, stirring constantly. Stir in flour-water mixture; cook until sauce thickens. Remove from heat and stir in bourbon.

Blueberry Strawberry Buckle _____

Makes 9 servings

½ cup butter *or* margarine at
  room temperature
1 cup sugar
1 egg
1 teaspoon vanilla
1½ cups all-purpose flour
1 teaspoon baking powder
1 teaspoon salt
½ cup milk
1 cup blueberries
1 cup sliced strawberries
½ teaspoon cinnamon
½ teaspoon nutmeg
  Sweetened whipped cream *or*
  vanilla ice cream, optional

Preheat oven to 350° F. Grease a 9-inch square baking pan. In a small bowl, cream ¼ cup of the butter and ½ cup of the sugar. Blend in egg and vanilla. In a small mixing bowl, stir together 1 cup of the flour, baking powder, and salt. Add dry ingredients to creamed mixture alternately with milk; stir until blended. Pour batter into prepared pan. Arrange fruit over batter. In a small bowl, combine remaining sugar, remaining flour, cinnamon, and nutmeg. Cut in remaining ¼ cup butter until mixture is crumbly. Sprinkle crumb mixture over fruit. Bake for 35 minutes. Serve with sweetened whipped cream or vanilla ice cream, if desired.

Rice Pudding

Makes 8 servings

1 quart milk
¾ cup sugar
4 eggs, beaten
1 teaspoon vanilla
2 cups cooked rice
½ teaspoon cinnamon
¼ teaspoon nutmeg
¼ teaspoon salt
1 cup golden raisins
   Light cream, optional

Preheat oven to 325° F. Butter a 2-quart baking dish. In a medium saucepan over medium heat, scald milk. Set aside to cool. In a separate bowl, beat sugar, eggs, and vanilla until well blended. Stir rice, spices, and salt into cooled milk. Stir egg mixture into rice mixture. Stir in raisins. Pour batter into prepared baking dish. Place baking dish in a large, shallow pan. Pour in hot water to a depth of 1 inch. Bake for 1 hour. Stir thoroughly. Bake an additional 30 minutes or until a knife inserted near the center comes out clean. Cool on a rack. Serve warm or cold in shallow bowls. Top with light cream, if desired.

Zabaglione

Makes 8 servings

8 egg yolks
6 tablespoons sugar
¾ cup Marsala
1 pint fresh raspberries

In a large, heatproof bowl, beat egg yolks until thick and lemon-colored. Gradually beat in sugar. Blend in wine. Place bowl over a pot of hot, but not boiling, water. Be sure bottom of the bowl does not touch water. Cook mixture, beating constantly, until mixture leaves sides of pan. Remove from heat. Divide berries among 8 sherbet glasses. Pour custard over berries. Serve warm.

Frozen Vanilla Custard

Makes 2 quarts

6 eggs, lightly beaten
2 cups milk
¾ cup sugar
2 tablespoons honey
¼ teaspoon salt
2 cups heavy cream
1 tablespoon vanilla

In a medium saucepan, beat eggs, milk, sugar, honey, and salt until well blended. Cook over low heat, stirring constantly, until the mixture thickens and coats a metal spoon. Cover and refrigerate until thoroughly chilled. Add heavy cream and vanilla; blend well. Pour mixture into a 1-gallon ice cream freezer can. Freeze according to manufacturer's directions.

Prune Coffee Cake

Makes 1 loaf

1½ cups pitted prunes
½ teaspoon cinnamon
¼ teaspoon nutmeg
1 teaspoon vanilla *or* 2
   tablespoons Armagnac
2 cups all-purpose flour
1 teaspoon baking powder
1 teaspoon baking soda
½ teaspoon salt
½ cup shortening at room
   temperature
1 cup sugar
3 eggs, beaten
   Grated peel of ½ orange

Preheat oven to 325° F. Grease and flour a 9 x 5-inch loaf pan. In a small saucepan, combine prunes, 1 cup water, cinnamon, and nutmeg. Bring to a boil over medium heat. Reduce heat, cover, and simmer for 15 minutes. Drain prunes; reserve liquid. Add water to prune liquid to make ½ cup, if necessary. Stir vanilla into prune liquid; set aside. In a medium bowl, stir together flour, baking powder, soda, and salt. In a large mixing bowl, cream shortening and sugar. Add eggs to creamed mixture, 1 at a time, beating well after each addition. Add dry ingredients to creamed mixture alternately with prune liquid. Stir in prunes and orange peel. Pour batter into prepared pan. Bake 1½ hours. Cool in pan 10 minutes. Turn out onto a rack to cool completely.

Rhubarb Kuchen

Makes 12 servings

1¾ cups flour
1 teaspoon baking powder
2 tablespoons sugar
½ teaspoon salt
½ cup butter
¼ cup chopped nuts
2 egg yolks, lightly beaten
2 egg yolks
2 cups sugar
½ cup flour
4 to 5 cups rhubarb,
   cut in 1-inch pieces
   Meringue

In a bowl, stir together flour, baking powder, sugar, and salt. Cut in butter until mixture is crumbly. Stir in nuts and egg yolks until well mixed. Press into the bottom of a 9 x 12-inch baking pan.

Preheat oven to 350° F. In a separate bowl, beat egg yolks. Add sugar and flour; stir until blended. Stir in rhubarb. Pour rhubarb mixture into crust. Bake 45 minutes. Remove kuchen from oven. Reduce oven temperature to 325° F. Top kuchen with Meringue. Bake for 10 minutes or until Meringue is delicately browned.

Meringue

4 egg whites
¼ teaspoon salt
¼ teaspoon cream of tartar
¾ cup sugar
1 teaspoon vanilla

In a deep bowl, beat egg whites until foamy. Add remaining ingredients; beat until stiff peaks form.

· Index ·